CN00860142

"**Cheryl White** is a ⟨
make this guide both highly
being simplistic. Packed with
writing achieves the difficult task of taking sensitive, often
challenging subject matter and convey it with a light touch and
a wonderful (often laugh out loud) humour. A brilliant guide
for those new to the subject and an informative reference for
practitioners. Highly recommended."

Louise Burford, Harley Street Practitioner.
www.louiseburford.com

"This entertaining, informative and lovingly supportive
book reminds me of the Hitchhikers Guide to the Galaxy. It
will make total sense to people who have experienced an EFT
and Matrix Reimprinting training. To those people who are
now living in the post-EFT parallel universe, where life is SO
different to how it was a day, week or a month ago. To those
of you who are so excited, you can't wait to tap on anybody or
anything that will stand still long enough. Welcome to my
world! And where was this guide when I needed it many years
ago as my whole world and life transformed?"

Sharon King, creator of Matrix Birth Reimprinting
www.magicalnewbeginnings.com

"Where was this book when I first learnt EFT??? I wish
this book had been available when I was starting my journey
of transformation from suffering with M.E to living my dream
life. Cheryl White has brought together in a fun yet
informative way all the topics that every EFT and Matrix

1

Reimprinting attendee will need in their days and weeks after undertaking their initial training. This book provides emotional understanding and practical support. Your initial questions will be answered and you will feel like a big comfort blanket has embraced that uncertain void of "what do I do now?" experienced by many after leaving the course."

Susie Shelmerdine, author, *Realise Your EFT Business Dreams*
www.susieshelmerdine.com

"This book is packed with a load of information for the newly trained but you read it without it ever feeling as though there's a load of information packed into a small space, as it reads so naturally.

Cheryl White is an observant and skilled wordsmith and she paints evocative, (and often humorous), pictures which will resonate with many.

I sincerely think it's a great 'little' book that can and will help people at the time they need it most. "

Fiona Truman, *creator of the MindMap™ Tapping Process*
www.mindmaptapping.com

"What an awesome read this is and one that I so wish I had back in the early days of training. Reading it you will feel understood, heard and supported. It will gently guide you to see your own potential, work through your own poop and help others to work through theirs if you put the advice into practice. Blasting apart any fears you may have as a practitioner and as a person as it's honest and to the point with a huge dollop of humour along the way. A must read for all new practitioners and even seasoned ones. Engaging throughout you will be glad you made the time to read"

Wendy Fry, author, Find You Find Love
www.wendyfry.com

"A beautiful well written book, easy to understand whilst cleverly intertwining therapeutic models from a counselling perspective!
Well done Cheryl, I love the book!!"

Balvinder Padda, Person Centred Counsellor

"A great in-depth look to the roller coaster ride if becoming a practitioner, written by the insightful Cheryl White's brilliant humorous penmanship. A must to read."

Penny Croal, Master Meta-Health Trainer
www.changeahead.biz

"So you've just qualified! What now? In this well-written, informative, no-nonsense and at times extremely funny book, Cheryl undertakes to explain the inevitable up and down journey you will have. I related to everything covered and strongly recommend this as an Essential Read, especially for all EFT newbies. There are many things that are not covered in your training course, which are expertly covered here. Cheryl is a well-seasoned therapist who has supported countless new practitioners, you will be glad she's supporting you on your journey too!"

Tahira Aziz, Regeneration Consultant
www.tahiraaziz.com

"I would have loved to have had a copy of this book when I first completed my training! It is entirely supportive of newly qualified practitioners and deals with many things that don't often get talked about - I'm thinking of that slightly lost feeling I encountered after completing my training when I felt different inside, but the world was still sort of the same. There are a lot of books out there about EFT, but this is the only one that is aimed at supporting practitioners directly. If you've recently trained, or are thinking of training, this book is worth reading."

Caroline Nairn, Psychotherapist, BA, PGDip (Psych), ADip (Psych), AAMET, UKCP, MBACP

www.carolinenairn.com

So Now I'm a Practitioner? Help!

Things to Know when Newly Qualified in EFT and Matrix Reimprinting

Cheryl White

Copyright

Title: So Now I'm a Practitioner? Help!

Subtitle: Things to Know when Newly Qualified in
              EFT & Matrix Reimprinting

Author: Cheryl White

Copyright © 2015 by Cheryl White: First Edition, 2015
Published in the UK

Special Thanks

In alphabetical order, special thanks go to Caroline Bellamy, Steve Blampied, Louise Burford, Penny Croal, Karl Dawson, Jennifer Florence, Caroline Nairn, Balvinder Padda and Fiona Truman all for proofreading or encouraging, or in some essential way supporting me and/or this little book. It is so wonderful to feel valued and appreciated by good people.

Important Disclaimer

This book is designed to provide information on ways to acclimatise after EFT or Matrix Reimprinting training.

It is sold with the understanding that the publisher and author are not engaged in rendering legal, medical or other professional services. If medical or other expert assistance is required, the services of a competent professional should be sought. It is not the purpose of this manual to reprint all the information that is otherwise available to new EFT or Matrix Reimprinting practitioners, but instead to complement, amplify and supplement other texts and/or face to face trainings. You are urged to read all the available material, learn as much as possible about your chosen energy therapy, interrelated therapies and practices, personal development and business and practice management, and tailor the information to your individual needs.

The purpose of this manual is to educate and entertain. The author shall have neither liability nor responsibility to any person or entity with respect to any loss or damage caused, or alleged to have been caused, directly or indirectly, by the information contained in this book.

Table of Contents

About the Author

In between running her own practice on the South Coast of England and the Brighton EFT and Matrix Reimprinting practitioner swap group, Cheryl White also manages the EFT practitioner test system for EFTMRA, having co-written the questions and designed the test format. She says the best bit is getting to say "Hi" to all the recent trainees at the very start of their journey.

Cheryl first discovered EFT in 2007 and is now a Matrix Reimprinting Practitioner and EFT trainer and devotes her spare time to befriending and encouraging new practitioners, answering their questions and providing emotional and practical support through various media. When very lucky, she says, she gets to kick back and assist at other people's trainings and help individual new trainees through their overwhelms and breakthroughs.

In a past life Cheryl worked for the BBC and in local government before successfully taking her LEA to court and suffering health issues in the process, ending up working in a golf-club kitchen during school hours, as "the only Mensan pot-wash, ever".

At the time of writing, Cheryl is also a proud member of AAMET and AMT.

Foreword

As an Emotional Freedom Techniques (EFT) Master and creator of Matrix Reimprinting, I have trained several thousand new EFT practitioners over the years.

Originally for AAMET (Association for the Advancement of Meridian Energy Therapies) and more recently for my own training academy EFTMRA (The EFT and Matrix Reimprinting Academy), I regularly train at least 200 potential new practitioners every year, face to face, nationally and internationally. This is beside teaching and mentoring my own elite team of new EFT and MR trainers and my work as author of two best-selling books with the usual variety of public speaking engagements and seminar interviews.

I am very pleased to be able to endorse and actively promote this small, witty and long overdue publication, which I can personally confirm covers most if not all of the post-training hiccups that new practitioners can experience, and does so in a warm, welcoming and light-hearted fashion. It is a deceptively easy read, quietly packed to the hilt with very real advice and information, and will be a welcome companion to any new practitioner who fears that they struggle alone with, for example, arranging swaps, or having a crush on their trainer.

Having trained for both EFTMRA and AAMET, and with a similarly close connection to Silvia Hartmann and the team at AMT, I can predict that this, Cheryl White's first book, will become a mainstay for new practitioners across the board.

Karl Dawson EFT Founding Master,
Creator of Matrix Reimprinting, Hay House Author

1.

Introduction

So you've passed your EFT practitioner exam (and possibly also Matrix Reimprinting), bought your insurance, maybe even ordered the business cards. Your life has changed beyond belief in the last few weeks or months and you're all fired up with a passion to make this a large chunk of your life's work . . . and you don't have a clue what to do next! At least I imagine that's the position you're in if you've picked up this book. Once upon a time, me too.

Imagine all the excitement; the first day of a packed training course run by EFT Master Karl Dawson, upstairs in a swanky hotel. He's pulled one or two of those icebreaker tricks of his, designed to unnerve the group and leave them in no doubt that emotional energy is registered on the physical level. We've all had a good chuckle about it, eventually, and now everyone is so much more relaxed that not only is each person happily saying a few words about themselves, some are just as happily ignoring any and all suggestions regarding brevity in the face of an impending tea-break.

And there I sit, feeling more and more like a fish out of water, blatantly the only attendee in a class of thirty psychologists, nutritionists, doctors and reiki masters to have no career, no formal qualifications and my personal pièce de résistance and 'three bags full', a muddle of special needs kids, debts up to the eyeballs, and self-confidence that had been under the steamroller so often, it had taken up residence an inch below the tarmac. I am (was) polyester, Primark and Poundland, surrounded by M&S and Jasper Conran, good shoes, good haircuts and good educations. Even my 'cheerful' was faux. Day two, I wore four inches of makeup. So I wouldn't cry.

That's enough of my story for now; it's only there to assure you that I've made pretty much every single one of the mistakes* in this book, personally and with flair. In fact, after setting up a closed Facebook group, now in its fourth year, specifically for providing support to new practitioners, I realised how often such matters are raised. Hence this offering.

It is my absolute hope that I can save you from one or two of the common early pitfalls and ease your path to success and confidence. With that in mind, it makes no difference whether you read this systematically or dip in and out to take only the parts that resonate with you. Enjoy.

*Technically there are no mistakes, only lessons. Get used to telling yourself that - there's a lot out there to learn, and it might as well be fun.

2.

'After the Fire'

Readjusting after Training

Training is pretty amazing, huh? Maybe you'd even call it intense? Whether the group you were in kept its dignity and composure or had its full share of tearful moments, I'm guessing that at least one of your heaviest emotional burdens saw this as its big chance, thrust its way to the fore and demanded your love and undivided attention right there on the spot. If needed, you left the room and went off with one of the training assistants to work privately until you felt able to return.

Whatever your motivations for attending, you've come away with some major shifts in your outlook and yet, after receiving your attendance certificate, skipping joyfully through the group photos and group hugs, high hopes, higher moods and truly fond farewells, you've stepped outside of that glorious atmosphere to find yourself slap-bang back in the middle of the so-called 'real' world with its sharp elbows and sharper tempers.

What now?

Here are some of the fleeting thoughts and experiences that may resonate with you. Short and sweet - they are not at all unusual and you are not at all odd, nor alone. At the end of this chapter there are also some essential self-care tips for smoothing the transition.

2.1

Why does my body hurt?

In a word, regeneration. It's all good, all part of the healing process, and it's actually the tail end of it too; a good marker that you are ridding yourself of the physical effects of a redundant belief.

Have you ever taken your shoes off after a long hard day, to realise how, within minutes, your feet just wouldn't go back in again even if you used a crowbar? All that time rushing around and yet it's only when you are safe to relax that things start to (briefly) hurt? Fleeting physical regeneration after an energy shift is exactly the same. Your body recognises that it is free of a restraint, and promptly sets about healing by swelling, relaxing, maybe aching. You just might feel a little uncomfortable, but it truly is a cause for celebration!

When you have held yourself under emotional tension over something for a long time, your excellent, wonderful, creative, adaptive body has continuously responded by producing the right chemicals and hormones to keep you 'on your toes', alert to the danger and ready to respond. The deeper and more intense the emotional healing has been, the more likely you are to feel something, as the chemical (epigenetic) element of that leaves your body.

Help it along - DRINK MORE WATER.

2.2

Why does my family seem worse than ever?

It is often true that people around you will be delighted by your new, more positive outlook and will be happy for you, so long as you don't expect them to have to make some sort of effort to accommodate any tiny changes of plan. It can also be true that some people will openly balk at the idea that things aren't simply going to trundle along just the way they always have. If someone digs in their heels and refuses to budge from the old dynamic, then this can be a cause of frustration and pain for both of you.

Even worse, life could carry on smoothly, with your nearest and dearest relaxed and supportive of your new found confidence and sense of self... and yet.... you could find yourself taking a long, hard look at them and feeling as though you have now completely outgrown them, or even that suddenly they have the most annoying character traits imaginable.

Although it's all essentially the same thing in the whole oneness of, well, stuff; just as a stick has two ends, this situation has two reasons.

Firstly, your own personal outlook has changed. On a conscious, tangible level you have undone some of your longer standing fears. You don't feel so restricted anymore.

More things seem possible, even natural and you are ready to translate these into practical action.

Here is a little story to try and explain. I was once told of a terrible old people's home. Someone I worked with had gone to visit this establishment, and immediately decided to find another place for their aging parent. The reason? As they sat waiting to speak to the Nursing Sister, one elderly lady with dementia was left screaming in absolute panic right there in the sunny communal living space. All she had done was walk into the corner of the room and then forget that there was anything at all behind her. All she could fathom was the wall in front of her, which, as far as she knew, went right round like a box; no way out, no escape. When a member of staff eventually came to help, they seemed overworked and unimpressed as if this particular lady went through this torment quite regularly. The attitude toward the patient seemed to be 'Stop being so frustrating'.

This is not such a far stretch from how we can accidentally treat our life partners, before we get a proper grasp on just how much growth and change we have undergone, during the training. If we are touched by the Apex Effect at all it may not be in denying the work that we've done or the transformation that we've gone through, but in wrapping our heads around just how restricted our idea of normality used to be, even this time last week. In effect, we get home to find our partners, who up until now matched us pretty well, are still facing the corner, still believing in the box that we used to think we shared and now can't begin to imagine. Whether they survive it stoically or in torment, they just can't see that there is a whole world right behind them.

It is quite possible to find ourselves horrified or even disgusted at the extent of their limitations and certainly frustrated and feeling a little bit trapped, as we have to choose between letting go, or staying attached as a couple and waiting or hoping for them to clue in.

Secondly, it's an energy thing. This is much better news than the first point.

You've released and let go of the energy of certain redundant beliefs, and wherever or whenever you made those beliefs, that energy had been running with you ever since. It's like a contract, an agreement, an advertisement to the universe that you hold the belief which makes you needy of certain things. In return the universe contracts to supply you with those things you need, the emotional and spiritual crutches that allow you to function whilst still holding on to the belief you were running.

Everybody needs to be needed, and yet when you go back home, so far as the belief you have now escaped, you no longer have any of the weaknesses that used to come out of that. Our partners are often way more in tune with us than they realise and so the atmosphere that enters a room with you will advertise that you no longer need 'whatever it was'. If 'whatever it was' (reassurance, a certain power dynamic?) was a major part of your relationship, or something they could provide that made them feel good about themselves, then, wow, you've just got yourself an uncertain, insecure and confused life partner. You in return find yourself living with the person they become under stress.

Maybe they can't see their way out of the box, yet, or even believe that a way out exists, but they instinctively know that you've got out and left them to experience it on their own.

So why is this better news? The same energy that advertises how you have changed or grown also advertises who you now are. Even if you can't see it yourself, while you remain connected to each other your partner has a choice; to dig in their heels and blame you for changing or to take your lead and grow too. They might even try doing both, but the decision of the subconscious is the one that will win. If they choose the latter, as you've already done the work, forged the path and lit it up for them, the transition can be surprisingly smooth.

Hang on in there. If it's bringing up bad emotions for you, then focus on them, on clearing your own issues, before making a move. At least then you'll be clear about things.

2.3

Why don't I know who I am anymore?

Yeah, you do really. No, honestly, you do. If it feels like the ground has moved, like you can't find a solid footing, then fair enough. Emotional ground level is a fallacy anyway; it's a construct we create for ourselves because we like to feel we know what's going on. We don't like to feel like we're floating the whole time. It helps to have something 'solid' to anchor ourselves to as it gives meaning to other fun concepts like direction and time.

So, on behalf of your inner self who signed up for this, sorry you're feeling a bit whooshy and sorry there aren't any travel sickness pills for this particular trip. Actually there's tapping, which works great, but as tapping got you into this situation I can't blame you if that sounds a bit like I just suggested hair of the dog for a hangover.

As a stop-gap, HeartMath breathing is a lovely exercise for attaining coherence without actually doing any work on specific issues. So is drinking lots of water. So is standing outside barefoot (but only on soil or grass and not in sub-zero temperatures). Grounding exercises like visualising roots can be useful too.

Just know that this is temporary - you threw a whole bunch of your preconceptions up in the air and now it's a matter of waiting to see which of them still have enough mass to respond to gravity and head gently back down to the ground. Meanwhile, you are stuck in a kind of dust vortex and not too certain how you think about things from one day to the next. You will definitely find a solid footing very shortly, except that it's not going to be the same one as before. Oh, and this time you won't fool yourself into thinking that it's necessarily permanent or even long-term.

I said sorry, already?

2.4

Do I have a crush on my trainer?

Here's the deal. IF you are asking yourself this question, the answer is 99.99% certain to be a clear and definite "No". No matter how hot and flustered and confused. Still. No. In fact I am naming this right now, in honour of the movie Despicable Me. it's the Agnes Effect.

Yes you are probably experiencing an onslaught of intense and childlike gratitude that just won't die down; each wave steeped in feelings of joy, delight, freedom, new opportunities, new possibilities and fresh amazement and all that other stuff that has some people shouting "Miracle!" and running through the streets. That in itself is a tremendous amount to cope with and quite possibly this may be the first time in your life that your little heart has had all its Christmases come at once. Even so, that state can (just about) exist without being targeted at an individual, and yet yours has convinced you that all the credit goes to your trainer. So here you now are, all flushed and embarrassed and feeling slightly annoyed at yourself and very awkward indeed because this all seems incredibly similar to affection (which is of course ridiculous, and you're just not like that, and one of you is far too old, and you're being silly, and anyway you don't even reserve such levels of attachment for your other half, and, and, and…)

My goodness, you haven't had this much faith in someone since you were, what; how old? Talking of Christmas, did you happen to still believe in Santa Claus or Fairy Godmothers back then, by any chance?

If you are asking yourself this question then I am guessing that you have just finished your level 1 or 2 EFT training, as this would not happen with Matrix Reimprinting or anything else that you could call advanced. More, at some point during this training you visited a childhood memory fraught with a fair amount of isolation and insecurity, and you associated. So there you were, feeling your younger self's intense discomfort, or describing what went on for that younger you by translating it through your 'now' body.

And now the person working with you is floundering, or at least, not quite confident yet.

And while you have your eyes closed and your head firmly in your childhood, they are making hand signals to the trainer to come over and help them with this.

So along comes the trainer and in a few brief seconds asks exactly the right question, makes exactly the right statement and generally makes it startlingly apparent to 5/6/7-year old you that they (you) are:

- understood,
- accepted,
- validated and
- just a completely okay person.

Yay!

And of course it's all rushed, and the point of that section of the training is not to go deep into a big memory, so there's more observation than regeneration and certainly no reimprinting.

And so now you're back out of that session. Except that you're not. Not really.

Hypnotists and hypnotherapists are well aware of a state-deepening trick called recursion (repeated trance induction) which involves putting you into a light trance, pulling you back out and then putting you back in again. The second trance hits harder, and the more often you are snapped in and out of trance state, the easier it is to go back down again, faster and deeper, as if the constant to-ing and fro-ing between conscious and subconscious gets your mind so fed up with the door slamming every five minutes, that it just props it wide open and leaves the two states connected until you're sure you're definitely done. More about recursion later.

Although we don't actually go into trance* during EFT, we do open the so-called alpha bridge and access both waking and subconscious brainwave patterns simultaneously, in order to allow us to visit memories with startling clarity. In a (safe, supportive, closely monitored) training environment we are by necessity pulled back out of that state by every tea break or discussion session before diving back in at the next practice, and it seems as if the same recursion rules can apply.

Your younger self, the one who was having a rotten time of it until your trainer came along and made him/her feel ever so grown up and special and safe, is therefore still in your energy field throughout the rest of the training. The door is still open between this reality and that specific event, and he/she is the one who is beaming a grin that would outshine the sun, jumping up and down and generally revelling in the belief that that big lovely grown up trainer person over there LIKES me!

I'm going to pick a single gender for a moment, just for simplicity, but all I have to say is this:

Love her. Know that it's her who feels a bit befuddled and star-struck. Know that you don't have to worry over whether you might have lost your mind, your pride or your normal taste in nooky.

Keep tapping. So one of your echoes has made and half-imprinted a new core belief about the amazing trustworthiness and reliability of your trainer. If you can see it for what it is, you'll work it out.

Have you seen the movie Despicable Me? Agnes, the youngest cartoon orphan, has a soft-toy unicorn, won at the fair.

Agnes = You (inner, little you)
Unicorn = Your poor trainer.
Nuff said.

We are actually all in some sort of trance to once extent or another every single day, but that's another story.

2.5

All my buried emotions are queuing up and shouting at me!

Yeah. That can happen.

You have survived X years on this planet, all the while stacking up all these big-T Traumas, small-t traumas, events and experiences, beliefs and vows and defences and decisions. You are still (relatively) sane and in one piece.

You're doing great. Under the circumstances, you're something of a superstar, actually.

Imagine, the problems we pack down and carry with us can behave a lot like sponge footballs in a tin, all under pressure. As soon as you give them some air, they seem to suddenly want to take up a lot more space. On the other hand, if they were going to all come out at once, they'd have done it before now and you'd be under sedation already, right? The fact is, the first one or two that you began to deal with during training have given you so much room for manoeuvre that it's become a lot easier to see any other issues that are ready and waiting to be dealt with.

That doesn't mean you have to deal with them.

Yet.

You *could* turn your back on energy therapies or on personal development in any incarnation at all, and simply go back to being who you were before (minus the issues you already shifted). You survived then, and you'll survive now, at least by any normal definition. You rock, you do.

Alternatively you could take your own sweet time, list them as part of a nice, long, specific Personal Peace Procedure and get methodical. Or you could work as fast as you wish on your own and in swap sessions, or mix it up by buying some sessions with more experienced practitioners.

So it's like, wow, this stuff really works, and your subconscious has started shouting "Wow, this stuff really works!" and now it's like you've finally turned up to your own metaphysical house clearance and finally brought the bin bags, and your subconscious is joyfully digging through cupboards for all the worst old trash and then under-arm bowling it straight at you.

It's not going anywhere until you decide, and meanwhile it's not doing any more harm than it ever did. If you do now happen to keep unexpectedly remembering more events that need attention, that's just your subconscious signing up and getting with the programme, putting your ducks in a row.

But, dang, you've got some real stuff there. Could be time to start with a list.

2.6

Is this going to happen every time?

No way!

There are two reasons I can say this and the first one is because of the nature of stress phases and regeneration phases and the way that they are proportional to each other. For example the longer you carry your heavy shopping (stress), the more floaty your arms feel when you finally get to put it down (regeneration).

The second reason I can say this is because of the nature of the training.

Energy therapy training is not a sudden miracle dropped into the still pond of your normal life. It can certainly feel that way, but actually it is part of your continuing journey. On all sorts of physical and spiritual levels, you already had direction and momentum which led you to this point, and on some level you have been gearing up to bring what is currently your biggest, most immediate trauma/crisis/drama to the party and deal with it in a quite dramatic make-or-break kind of way; during the training, in a corner, in a rush. You are in control, and you are doing great.

That's wonderful! That is also, ideally, what is NOT going to happen when you run your own practice, ever. Short of taking a re-sit, or attending a convention or other training event where major shifts can take you by surprise, you will normally create an environment where issues can be approached more gently, more methodically, and over more time and more sessions, with space either side for warming up to it first and then making sure your client is grounded and fully present at the end of the session.

2.7

Essential Self-Care Tips

Have Patience

Determine to forgive yourself, and everybody else too. Know that the amazing spiritual high you felt by the end of the training is, very often, physically unsustainable. In fact, the more a person's subconscious relishes the chance to get down to business and do their own work, the more rapidly they might lose that rosy glow and show signs of the task they've set themselves. If their post-training behaviour shocked you, then it shocked you; that's all. Send them love. Hearts on sleeves need extra love.

Drink Water

On an epigenetic level, you are changing your hormonal make-up and releasing biochemical stuff that was pre-ordered and is now surplus to needs, from your muscles and other tissues. As it gets evicted from your body, don't let it clog up your kidneys or anything else. Help it along.*

*Remember to sip water slowly during the day. The average sedentary adult will require 2 – 2.5 litres of fluids per 24 hour period. This figure will vary according to weight and lifestyle – don't overdo it, either!

Be Happy With Occasional Small Aches and Pains

By which I mean the odd lousy night's sleep after a major cognitive shift. The bigger the circus, sometimes the more noise when it leaves town. At least you know it's upped sticks and evacuated, and that the next lot to go is unlikely to be quite so big, or make quite such a din about it.

KEEP TAPPING!

Formally, informally, consciously, absent-mindedly, particularly, generally... just tap.

3.

Getting Over the Honeymoon

Making EFT a Habit

The most important step you can take is to make energy therapy a part of your daily routine. If you want to change even the tiniest part of the world, you need to care for the carer, or, as a kindly GP once put it to me "Everything you love and care for is under your circus tent, and you are the only supporting pole. Look after the pole."

The journey you are on has several way-stations. Some you will skim through without a second glance, some will involve slowing right down and taking stock. The object of this section of the book is to help you avoid coming to a dead halt. This chapter also presupposes that you know what a PPP is and are using yours to full effect. If not, it's covered again in the Useful Tools section.

So far, we've covered two stages:

- Realising the power of these methods, and
- Watching as your subconscious joins the party and starts volunteering new 'urgent' projects.

Coming up we've got:

- Getting used to working on big, dramatic things.
- Getting fed up with working on big, dramatic things.
- Redefining why you tap #1.

- Getting used to working on small, mundane things.
- Getting fed up working on small, mundane things.
- Redefining why you tap #2.

- Getting used to working on your passions!
  (That's as far as I've got...)

The reason I say that some of these may not be an issue for you is because it depends on how you experienced the training. Obviously, on a rational, surface level you took in all the information about protocols such as tearless trauma and sneaking up on the problem, or if you learned Matrix Reimprinting then also more advanced methods of keeping out of the picture and maintaining personal and professional safety and distance.

Whether you incorporate much of that information in your default method of practice, just yet, can rely heavily on the levels of exhilaration and transformation you experienced after being triggered during the training and rushing off to go through an emergency-crisis-overload mini session.

Yes, the trainer and helpers are experts and comfortable dealing with extreme reactions, overwhelm, PTSD, severe trauma, abreaction and whatever else can get thrown at them in such a situation.

No, this is not how they run their private practices and not what you should be aiming for in yours. You wouldn't expect your local GP to run his surgeries like a field-hospital surgical tent in the middle of a war zone. At least, not unless that's where you happen to live, and not unless all your headaches are always going to be caused by something requiring emergency surgery or amputation.

Yes, I fully understand that this observation may make no difference at all to your gleefully enthusiastic subconscious. So go work on all your own dramatic things, just please don't start to feel that doctoring might be pointless once your stitches are out.

3.1

Getting used to working on big, dramatic things

How you settle into this phase of the journey very much depends on your personality and also on outside factors like the amount of experience you have with other therapies and the amount of personal development work you are already used to.

Hopefully, your amazing experience during training has inspired you to work on being rid of all the issues and events that keep coming back to haunt you. However if you are like me, like I was, uptight and used to putting others first, used to mothering everyone and putting yourself last; if you cope by diversion, by focussing the world on the needs of others to hide the pain and shame of your own, then this one could be a bit of a culture shock.

Diversionary coping strategies will certainly make you a learning experience for your swap partners, although you are not as alone as you think, and that's a really important point to make.

The difficulty can arise when you are so embarrassed or frozen by one or more fears that even though they desperately need resolving, you feel unable to readily trust another new practitioner.

Officially - go with your gut; trust yourself. If you fear that you will be judged for your issues, or that someone will betray your confidence, then do not let anyone tell you different. If you have such a fear then not only is that (eventually) something else to tap on, but for some reason it would appear that these situations turn up in your life more often than not.

It doesn't matter one jot whether this is through divinely repeated lessons or law of attraction, or any other law, Murphy's included. What matters is that you will only get the most out of a proper session when you are ready and willing to be fully invested and to do the work.

There are ways forward through this. You could pay a more advanced practitioner to work with you. If confidentiality is your issue, this will make the boundaries very clear and you may feel more relaxed with someone who obviously has a functioning business and a reputation to maintain as a practitioner.

If you are ashamed of your fears, so hypersensitive to mockery or so judgmental of yourself for being potentially childish that confessing seems unbearable, you can specifically put feelers out for someone willing to 'work blind'. Again at the outset this is likely to be someone a little more advanced than you, as this takes a confidence in their own ability, both to monitor your progress by physical/aural/energetic signs alone, and to know when to interject. As this method of working also does away with any concerns over confidentiality, it may be possible to find someone ready to assist as part of a swap, especially if you ask in one of the Facebook groups.

3.2

Getting fed up with working on big, dramatic things

The moment when constantly rooting around in your psyche looking for a trauma to work on begins to feel a bit 'off' is actually one which deserves a major celebration.

If you have had quite an eventful past, and if your subconscious has been gleefully chucking fairly tearful or intense memories at you on a regular basis every time you need something to work on, then it may eventually start to feel as if there must be something inherently wrong with you.

Then, if you stand up for yourself (Yes! Result! You stood up for yourself!), it can be very easy to flip that thought on its head and decide that no, in fact, there must be something wrong with EFT.

I know from experience that at this point in your development it can feel as if all this clearing of old trauma is a bit like playing God, like being expected to throw your entire house-of-cards life out with the garbage and create your own designer version of yourself instead, without any rules or guidelines. Like being given a totally clean slate on the understanding that nothing about your original 'you' was actually good enough, and, and. . . EFT, how dare you!

What is actually happening is that all your hard work is simply showing more benefits than you expected so soon. To

41

use a training analogy, you've chopped down enough trees and now suddenly a whole chunk of the forest has gone, one that you never even got to touch. You thought you had a map, and now the whole terrain has changed.

Not to call you in any way a victim before this point, but suddenly you have a whole lot more confidence in (and personal approval of) yourself, and a whole lot less inclination to submit to a sense of needing to be rescued. If you left training and immediately established a habit of only ever dealing with events that carried a high emotional charge, you risk associating EFT with getting all dramatic, which would be a pity. That's called throwing the baby out with the bathwater.

This is the first point where many students mistakenly decide that perhaps EFT isn't for them after all, and take a break from tapping that just gets longer and longer until suddenly you might as well call it permanent. Please, don't stop.

3.3

Redefining why you tap #1

As we've established, the habit you have adopted of working on 'big' dramas every single time, can encourage you to feel quite exasperated. What you experience when you physically growl at the thought of digging up more dirt on yourself just for a swap session, is only the next onslaught of incongruent beliefs, all of which stem from other energy memories. You've begun to move on from issues of life or death, to issues of identity and worth and belonging and anger.

Now would be a perfect time to find out a little bit about Maslow's Hierarchy of Needs, because it describes the stack of human personal goals in a neat graphic. Essentially nobody can afford to exert energy on higher pursuits when they need to be urgently focussing on the life and death stuff. Sort out the basics, and then there's room for prettier pursuits. You just moved up a floor or two on Mr Maslow's pyramid, is all.

There's a whole section going into greater detail about Abraham Maslow later in this e-book.

Here's a trick: Change tack.

EFT tapping will shift some sort of blocked energy even if it's used globally without a specific event or feeling in mind. This is because it will work on whatever is in the energy body at the time. We always have lots of stuff in our energy bodies, except we're so used to it we can't tell; we call it normality. Because it works like this too, you can decide to simply focus on making the tapping part into a habit. Not the hour-long Skype sessions with concerned friends, not the HeartMath and grounding, not even the ceremonial placement of drinking water and tissues. Just the tapping.

3.4

Getting used to working on small, mundane things

By all means keep up with your swap sessions, tapping circles, mentoring work, and if you have them, client sessions.

If you would like to take a break from deeper work on your own account, would like to quit digging the skeletons out of the closet and turn your mind to smaller, more decorative changes, then this switch is probably going to be quite a smooth transition. The same applies if you would simply like to invest your energies in having a happy day here in real time.

If you want to continue with the investment you've made into EFT and yourself, but really can't hack the concept of having to stop and focus on something you'd like to see the back of, then all you need is a small commitment to yourself to make time for a round or two *on nothing in particular*.

Here is one possible method:

Let's say you commit to two to five minutes of EFT tapping per day and no more than that. Perhaps only in the bathroom, perhaps just before you brush your teeth in the morning, perhaps facing the mirror. Don't even let it matter what your subject is:

- Even though the sink needs a clean
- Even though I don't know what to tap on
- Even though I have to fill the car up today

- Even though I look like a right bl**dy wreck in this mirror
- Anything.

Make a little checklist of dates, or hang up a calendar where you go to tap and tick off the day every time you've done at least two rounds. Don't sweat it if you miss the odd one. On the day that you look back and realise you have at least three full weeks, 21 days of consecutive ticks, the actual physical element of tapping will be well on its way to zooming past habit status and into muscle memory.

If people stop tapping this far along their journey, it's generally because they've not thought of giving themselves permission to take things so lightly.

Don't let a lifetime spent believing things have to be hard work for little benefit, get in the way of this being joyfully simplistic and easy, for a massive return.

3.5

Getting fed up with working on small, mundane things

Ha! Got you. So far as I am aware, this doesn't actually happen. Feeling all deliciously benign and non-judgmental and uninvested in those tiny everyday situations that used to get you muttering under your breath, is far, far too addictive. It is also the mainstay of spiritual growth and allows you to witness how much your ego is losing the power to spoil your day.

'Getting fed up' is also an ego construct, it's a condition born of aggravation, fear and various other undercurrents, of being problem-centred instead of solution-centred. When it transforms, it becomes 'Growing beyond'.

Taking a step to grow beyond something is a beautiful, positive inspiration to experience more, without any need to judge what you were previously doing as in any way inadequate.

Time to stretch those wings.

3.6

Redefining why you tap #2

I don't know how else to put this, so this is going to be a really short section.

We are not built to stagnate, we can't do it. It is in our nature, in the core of our very being, to dream, wish, create, hope and imagine and to keep growing.

If you are reaching the top of Maslow's pyramid (for lack of another graphic example, just now), if you feel safe enough and established enough to be turning your creativity to hopes and possibilities, then you can already see that energy therapy is a gift, perfectly fashioned to cut the cords that restrain you and your dreams from reaching the stratosphere.

If you used to compare EFT to magic healing paste for the emotionally half-dead, you might as well now compare it to super turbo fairy dust. Or rocket fuel. (Just trying to be gender inclusive here). Take your pick.

3.7

Getting used to working on your passions!

Perhaps you will wake up one morning, totally inspired, and simply know what it is that you want to do with your life.

Otherwise, you will find little inspirations, smaller hopes and dreams, start to pop into your mind, to the extent that you don't really know which one to focus on, what direction to head off in.

S.M.A.R.T. is a wonderful acronym to borrow from the world of business, if you need a little extra tool to help you decide where to start. There have been various incarnations, but the one for this goes:

SMART:

Specific, Measurable, Attainable, Relevant, Time-bound.

- **Specific** - Easy! We energists love being specific. Make a precise statement about what you would like to achieve.

- **Measurable** - How will you know when you've got there?

- **Attainable** - Quick reality check - no dreams about barn dancing with the pixies?
- **Relevant** - This should be 'Resonate'! Does this resonate with you? Is it in your truth?
- **Time-Bound** - Go on, get scary, take this out of the clouds and make a clear intention on when you would like it to manifest.

So far as being specific (and to get the ball rolling) how about:

"I want five full-paying clients a week, all in long term contracts, all taking 90-minute sessions",

"I want the perfect consultation room" (describe colour, dimensions, location, furnishings).

"I want to go out and give a live demonstration and talk, all on my own."

. . . and breathe. Does it really resonate with your sense of passion? When do you want it? How will you know?

And what's stopping you? Where in your body is the fear (or the hysterical laughter)?

Have fun.

4.

Swaps

How to Survive Them

Swap partners are essential, and swap partners are human. Unless one of you is supremely confident, or has already done a truckload of work, it is highly unlikely that any of your earliest swap partners will settle into a truly constant arrangement with you for the coming years. Even the next six months could be a stretch. And it's all perfect.

This is not said in order to pour cold water on anything, quite the opposite. It really helps, when an agreement falters to a close, to realise that nothing is cast in stone, that people grow and change and that this is not only to be expected, it is also a sign that the two of you have each upheld your end of the bargain, by helping each other to move forward and move on.

Further into this chapter I have described three very practical reasons to continue with a habit of swapping sessions. However, it may be of use here at the outset of your journey while the thrill is so new, to look closely at the CPD (continuous personal development) requirements of your chosen professional body or bodies.

Although you may want to prioritise a strong sense of rapport when choosing your swap partners and to maximise the growth you experience when taking the role of client, sometimes it helps to remember that Association codes of practice cannot specify that you benefit from a swap system, only that you 'show up'. Sometimes it's about keeping on keeping on.

4.1

Early swaps and why they (sometimes) go wrong

Just for fun, let's say you and your fantastic swap partner met in a metaphorical shared hole in the ground, and for visualisation purposes, I'm thinking edge of the desert and all very Spaghetti-Western.

However wonderful or transformative or head-spinning your training was, for some reason, out of all the people there, you both latched on to each other. This is because you resonated with each other, you represented slightly more familiar territory than others on the same course. You were to some emotionally important extent on the same wavelength and facing the same issue or issues - the hole.

Working together to lift yourselves up seemed obvious and perfect and a gift. In fact, because of the commitment to swap sessions, you were able to get out of that hole and re-orient yourselves. But what now? At this point, it may turn out that one of you has a heart that leads to the mountains and the other yearns for the town. Or the river. Or the . . . something else.

The following is an absolute worst case scenario, but when things go wrong it can simply be because only one of you is innocently skipping your way to happiness like Julie Andrews in full song, while the other can be crumpling in a corner with rejection and feeling like Norma No-mates (which, by the way is just another deep core belief queuing up for attention). Let's deal with that one first:

4.2

Feeling rejected when it ends

Sticking with this rapidly disintegrating image for just one more point, if you are the one feeling rejected, it feels to you as though the other person dumped on your unspoken commitment to deal with each other's junk and has now taken off without a backward glance, while you were still patting yourself down, checking your pockets and re-tying your shoelaces. It would have been nice to shake hands and say "See you later", yes? Or to make sure it wasn't anything you said, or that ten-day-down-a-hole armpit whiff... hmm? Nothing about your secrets or self-judgments about 'who you really are' that made them want to politely edge away?

Counsellors and NLP practitioners refer to this situation as breaking rapport (more on that later), and it can feel absolutely devastating, more so when the habitual swaps have set up a recursive system. The funny thing about hypnotic recursion is that the subject (that's you) tends to get into the habit of automatically going deeper into a state of relaxation during successive therapy sessions, on the basis that the deeper you go, the better you feel when you do the work and come out, and the better you feel, then next time the deeper you go.

Another definition of recursion comes from psychologists and cognitive behaviour therapists who refer to 'Recursive Cognitive Structures', which is a fancy way of saying 'vicious circles' (a fancy way

which also uses title case, because everyone in the mainstream loves a
TLA or Three Letter Acronym. A good TLA is a bit like a magic
wand - nothing to do with the actual 'magic' and everything to do with
having something to wave around.)

So where were we? Oh yes; you. So there you are, still firmly habituated to your swap sessions with this one particular person, at this one particular time every week, which has started to become, from your perspective, a reliable symbiosis and a big fat part of your comfort and safety zone. In fact it's becoming kind of easier to go away and cope magnificently with the inordinate amount of stress and pressure you habitually live under for the rest of the week, because this chance to change your life forever is going to turn up again same time, same channel. It's your lifeline, your air. You NEED this, although you've probably not realised, let alone admitted it to yourself.

At the point when, for whatever unexpected reason, the arrangement breaks down and just doesn't happen anymore, you can still automatically continue to experience recursion for a while. This is a fancy way of saying your body-clock and emotions have got into a habit so that your inner Echoes (Energy Consciousness Holograms or in this case inner stressed children) come pushing their way to the fore ready to have some healing attention that just ~ ain't ~ gonna ~ happen. You're feeling the vacuum and mourning the loss.

This can happen whenever you have an interruption to a habit - perhaps you skip church, or your evening class stops for half term, or you forget to phone your mum, however, this is a potentially more emotionally volatile situation. Your inner kids, especially the ones that need attention (as client) or need to be needed (as practitioner) can turn into Rugrats, tool up, and threaten to beat you up or start shooting your mouth off on your behalf.

As to your swap partner and very nearly best-friend-for-life, there they were, gone.

Sucks to be you.

On the other hand, it's all perfect. So what if your inner five-year-old is throwing toys and wants his or her bestest mending grown-up back? At least if he/she is throwing a tantrum and not crushing on them, that's some sort of progress. It's also true that school age kids sometimes have an amazing propensity to make a new and different BFF* on a weekly basis.

*BFF: Best Friend Forever.
Keep tapping.

4.3

Feeling elated when it ends

Okay, so maybe you're not feeling elated exactly, more like completely normal, (plus or minus a weight or two off your mind from all that tapping) and totally unaware of the devastation going on behind you. Tra-la-la, and all that.

Or maybe, if we turn this on its head very slightly, you might be just a teensy bit aware of a certain amount of fuss, but find yourself mostly concerned about whether the person you were recently dealing with is, or ever has been, remotely normal. Well, not 'normal' in the way you are, anyhow.

Hmm, normal, remind me what that is, again?

The way to look at it is this: at least one of you (and it could be either*) is unconsciously acting out the needs of echoes. At least one of you is presently responding to the world or to this situation in particular, straight from the defensive hindbrain. Assuming you are both committed to energy work and to personal transformation, who do you suppose is revving up for the biggest growth spurt?

(*It's always both to a greater or lesser degree, in fact it's always everybody, otherwise you'd have all the growth potential of a house brick, and where would be the fun in that?)

4.4

What to do about either situation

I cannot stress this often enough - keep tapping. Keep tapping and keep owning that you tuned in to something uncomfortable deep within your own psyche, whether that's inclining you to act out or simply to feel really uncomfortable. Get working those finger points, every single time it interrupts your day.

Get on Facebook and find someone else to work with. Better still, start a secret interview process, find a dozen 'someone else's and do yourself a bit of swap-partner speed-dating. Get cracking with that Personal Peace Procedure (hit list). If you're lucky, you'll even have found a few more things to add to that, after the learning curve you just went through.

Really useful rule of thumb:

If one person does something to affect you, once, it might not be your problem. Not your circus, not your monkeys, as the saying goes. If more than one person does this, or it in any way happens to you more than once, it is, in fact, definitely and decidedly 'your problem'. Even if your actual problem is simply that you find this sort of thing to be 'a problem'.

Yup.

4.5

Three Really Good Reasons to Swap, Swap, Swap

There are three reasons to swap, and I must admit I love it when systems function in threes. Three sides make a triangle and triangles are the most stable shapes in existence.

These three interdependent reasons are continuous clearing, continuous learning and diminishing the ego.

Continuous Clearing:

The more of your own past experiences you resolve, the more balanced and relaxed (ergo healthy), positive, focussed, magnetic and stable you will be. At the same time, you will find yourself borrowing benefits less often and less dramatically when working with both swaps and clients.

Continuous Learning:

The more you relax and submit to other people's ways of running a session, the more you will become aware of your own tastes and your passion (and therefore niche). The more you experiment and share in the safety of swap sessions, the more you will increase your skill-set for pre-framing, reframing, holding the space, grounding your client, changing tack and responding appropriately to different situations, personality types and learning styles.

Diminishing the Ego:

The more you learn to trust the process, trust yourself, and most importantly trust your client to be on their own perfect journey, the more you learn to let go of any ego issues that keep you attached to a preferred outcome. It can be so heart wrenching, if, for example, you have tendencies toward rescuing others (see Karpman's Drama Triangle) or needing to be perfect, to find out that you have no idea whether the client benefited from your session or not.

It's just as hard to resist the temptation to lead, hint, nudge and put words in their mouth if you allow your ego to attach your own personal ideal of an outcome to somebody else's journey. The more you diminish your ego in this situation until you are truly listening, truly present and without a pre-set agenda, the more real benefits you will experience and bring to your clients.

Every one of these is such a privilege.

4.6

Swap Rules

How to play nicely with other people's children

Once you are up and running, most of these suggestions (if not all) will seem like common sense.

Matters are subtly different when you are starting out because the tendency is always to choose first swap partners from the group in which you trained, which gives you a lot to talk about and the potential for a really good friendship.

Friendships generally involve encouragement and commiseration, sympathising and empathising, sharing off-topic news and asking for advice (and feeling obliged to give some). Shared experience, particularly transformative experience, also encourages bonding, and bonding is an emotional investment in the other person's welfare.

Of course, not a single one of those belongs anywhere near a professional client/practitioner dynamic, so if friendly chat is going to become a part of your regular meet-ups or Skype appointments, it's going to be really important to have a pre-agreed indicator that the 'session proper' is about to start. As to your emotional investment in the other's welfare, perhaps the smoothest way to practice keeping your ego out of the way would be to decide to have faith.

Faith that this person is on their own right track. Faith that it's all happening at the perfect speed.

There can be a surprising number of opportunities to make contradictory assumptions about how the sessions will run, if you try and wing it, so it is for the two of you to set your own rules together. Only one rule is set in stone and that is the matter of absolute confidentiality. Imagine being desperate to heal a traumatic event, yet surrounded by practitioners you no longer dare to trust, because of careless sharing by one person with their L-plates on.

So, items you might want to clarify before working with another practitioner are:

1. The times you are going to 'meet'.
2. How long your meet-up will last each time.
3. How much of that time you will give to actual practice, at a minimum.
4. Whether you are going to swap both ways within the one meeting or alternate meetings.
5. If you both like a friendly catch-up before you begin, when exactly does the session and, therefore, the confidentiality, start? Right at the outset, or only when you start tapping? A difference in understanding on this point can cause real heartache.
6. If or how the session will be recorded and whether or not you share a copy with each other.
7. Is your session completely private, or is it likely to be interrupted?

I've experienced sessions where halfway through, when we are deep into the emotive and personal stuff, the other person's teenager or partner has popped their head around the door to say that they were going out, or to see how much longer we were going to take. A surprising number of new therapists set up their laptops in the kitchen and I once was deep into my turn as client, making some real cognitive connections when an odd noise broke the state. I asked what had happened and the lady said "Oh it's just my (teenage offspring) making a sandwich. Keep going, he/she'll be gone in a minute."

It's usually for a much smaller reason, but sometimes a swap-partner-client will jump back out of rapport and temporarily stop the session. The most important and gracious question you as the practitioner can ask after the session, is "What did I fail to do?" or "Is there anything I could have done better?".

It may be that you started leading or taking control of the session, or it may be that you introduced something unexpected that you neglected to pre-frame. Be nice to your client. Be the one to take responsibility and ask for feedback. They want their session and they want their issue to be dealt with and they will have insights for you on how to hold the space for someone like them. If this is allowed to happen, they end up feeling heard and you end up more skilled.

It is never the place of the swap partner acting as client to ask those same questions. However, a swap-client could stop things being too one-sided by asking "What did I do to challenge you?"

There is no such thing as a 'difficult client', only a client who challenges your current skill-set, and from this perspective whether as client or practitioner, both partners gain tremendous individual benefit from the same session.

5.

Useful Tools

Never mind the clients, these are for you!

Moving right along, to:

5.1

PPP - Personal Peace Procedure

What it is, how to use it, and how to keep it going

When you are told about the PPP in your first training, it is described as a list of specific events in your past which carry a negative emotional charge for you. The idea is that you make your list, you score the SUDs levels on each specific event, and then you start clearing them one by one, adding any new ones you think of to the back of the list.

If all your problems are all one-offs, all out of character, unusual and along the lines of 'My next door neighbour saw my bin lid in the street and he still reversed his car over it', then great, you'll easily build an initial list.

If your next door neighbour also generally behaves in disturbing ways a lot of the time, publicly and to others, without making you feel isolated, then it's going to be pretty easy to start a new PPP list or subsection entitled 'My Neighbour Needs Help' or 'My Neighbour The Psychopath' (or something a little less polite) and to recall a list of specific events that bring you to this conclusion. In fact this would very likely end up as a perfect example of those times when, going back to the training 'trees and forests' analogy, you clear the energy from some of the items to then discover that a great many related issues and events have also lost their power and their SUDs levels, without your obvious intervention.

If, however, your next door neighbour happens to have an inherent skill for isolating people before playing his or her power games, and if you are nearing the end of your tether with this, it is quite likely that the only statement you can come out with that holds any importance at all for you would be something like "My Neighbour Hates Me" or "My Neighbour Is Out To Get Me".

Sure, if you were pushed you could cite some examples for your list, but if for safety's sake you have generalised about his/her behaviour so that you won't make yourself vulnerable by accidentally treating them like, ooh, like they have a good side, or a soul or something… in this instance any stab at a PPP list is likely to be just as non-specific as the heading, and begin along the lines of "He/She always does (this), and always does (that), never does (the other) and always waits until nobody's looking to (something else)".

It's okay. It's perfect. Think of these as chapter subheadings and give yourself permission to work globally on each one. Yes, a PPP is ideally specific, but 'My Neighbour' as a global topic is still very valid for chasing the pain and sneaking up on the problem. Get your overwhelm and emotional charge down, and you will find that individual events and examples start to present themselves, after all.

When you use a Personal Peace Procedure, you are being your own practitioner. Give yourself the same space and compassion and faith that you would give to any other long-term client.

It's a good idea to keep your list beside you when you work on yourself in a swap setting too, as intriguing or diverting side issues will often come up mid-session when you are the client. If you have somewhere to scribble them down for later, they become much less likely to take your work off at a tangent.

5.2

Abraham Maslow - Hierarchy of Needs

Abraham Harold Maslow (1908-1970) studied "positive human qualities and the lives of exemplary people". In 1954, aged 46 he published his Hierarchy of Needs. Maslow recorded the highest state of being as 'Self Actualization', a state where the person desires to reach their full potential.

Maslow wanted to show how certain basic needs would have to be met, in order for someone to afford themselves the luxury of personal development.

Maslow's Hierarchy is drawn as a pyramid to emphasise how each level from the ground up is an essential foundation or precursor to the next level.

This is especially pertinent when looking at the way that your personal work will develop over time. The nearer the bottom of the triangle you could position an old event, the more likely it is to demand your attention to the exclusion of events from a higher layer.

Life-threatening occurrences and anything to do with your basic drives, i.e. the physiological issues, will come first. On average, most new trainees seem to begin by discovering a number of forgotten events where their safety felt threatened. As these issues are dealt with, so it becomes possible for issues and goals relating to higher states of being to come to the fore.

After "Will I live?" and "Am I safe?" come issues around "Am I loved and wanted?" then "Am I valuable and valued?" and finally "What are my dreams and what's holding me back?"

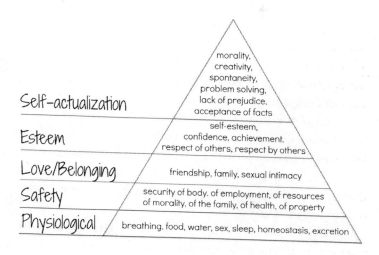

This maps quite neatly over the developmental stages in chapter 2, on making EFT a habit. Looking at Maslow's pyramid it is easy to see how, once most traumatic issues of basic safety are resolved, there is room to assess whether you are loved and valued, and to start to recognise yourself as definitely lovable and valuable (another reason why the traditional EFT set-up phrase can be such a neat litmus test).

According to Wikipedia trauma is "a type of damage to the psyche that occurs as a result of a severely distressing event". I'm just going to break that down a little bit.

Meta-Health practitioners have an acronym for severely distressing events - they call them an UDIN. UDIN stands for Unexpected, Dramatic, Isolating, and No coping strategy. The word psyche comes from the Greek psykhe, which means "the soul, mind, spirit, or invisible animating entity which occupies the physical body".

So now our definition of trauma is "Any type of damage/alteration/limitation to the soul which happened due to something unexpected and dramatic, a UDIN event that we can point to".

It seems to me that it is only as we heal, as we work our way back up Maslow's Hierarchy, we stop thinking of energy therapy as simply a tool for repairing extreme damage or trauma and start thinking of it as a tool for unwrapping our true and wonderful potential.

The Hierarchy of Human Needs is a basic mainstay of modern client-centred counselling.

5.3

Karpman Drama Triangle

If you know about the drama triangle, then you know a little bit of transactional analysis, so that's nice. It is also used in psychology and psychotherapy.

Stephen Karpman published this as part of an article in 1968.

The concept is that when we relate to each other, we tend to take on one of these three generalised roles of persecutor, rescuer or victim, so that in any interplay between three people, each would take on a different part within the dynamic.

Although it is quite possible to switch around depending on the situation, every one of us has a preferred default position that we gravitate towards. Because we are all susceptible, the strongest character will often draw others into their game and the task of a skilled practitioner is to keep their ego out of the mix by recognising this tendency in themselves and others and refusing to play along.

Each position involves protesting the condition, whilst at the same time, getting some sort of payoff out of staying right there, so plenty of hidden benefits or secondary gains.

Victim says, "Poor me, I'm useless, I'm a victim, it's not my fault and I'm blameless so I'm safe; love me no matter what."

Persecutor says, "I'm in the right, I know what's best and I have the power."

Rescuer says, "I'm good, I'll help. I'll let you manipulate me into taking on responsibility because then I'll be accepted."

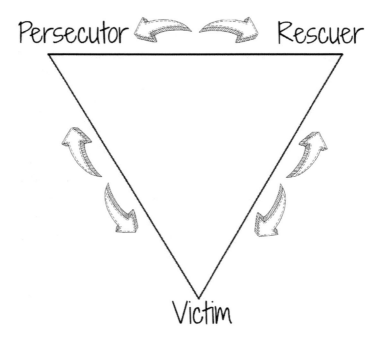

Although most examples are fleeting and far less extreme, we can all think of one or two pushy people who are very comfortable always being the only one in the right, as well as a few 'professional victims' who love it when everyone else treats them as ineffectual. In fact being 'of a type' doesn't make us blind to it in others, and we can all also think of one or two 'burning martyrs' who feel most at home wandering around perfecting a benign smile like an exhausted earth angel who's just pulled a double shift...

Most of us in the caring professions hit the trail as habitual rescuers. All of us have played all three roles at some point.

We start out needing to be needed.

It has to be said that stepping outside of this dynamic in order to perform the role of practitioner does not involve becoming some sort of disinterested robot. Quite the opposite. The wish to help is a wonderful thing, however behaving as a rescuer, or as psychologists also say, 'wounded healer', has another layer.

Put simply, it involves a decision to act, and to do so from a misplaced assumption that we happen to know the best outcome for the client. Once we truly believe this, it then becomes an almost irresistible urge to push the client towards seeing things our way, and, bam, your ego is not only back in the room, it's banging drums and shouting at people.

Be aware of this as you begin your swap sessions. Rescuer tendencies are what make us, as practitioner, burst to fill a silence or to lead our client, or to become invested in a specific outcome. The rescuer's need to be accepted (and not weak) can also make us, as client, devious in avoiding clearing our own stuff.

It's just worth knowing.

5.4

Overwhelm and overrun - the NLP Box

Overwhelm, at least high emotion wrapped in a high sense of urgency, is much more common when your EFT, energy therapy or other personal development practice is a new thing. Or vice-versa; it really is a chicken and egg scenario. Which came first, the learning or the need?

Finding yourself in sessions ('real' or 'swap') that seem to hit a new goldmine of emotional overwhelm in the last five minutes of the allotted space, is also a pitfall of 'being new', one that no longer happens to you as practitioner once you have confidence that it won't.

Both are 'morphic field' issues. Your morphic field is a pretty term for the stuff you've got going on, the issues you carry with you.

It all fits, or, as some would say, it's all perfect.

If it happens to feel less 'perfect' and more 'perfect storm', then there are any number of steps you can take to safely wrap up a session that is blatantly in the middle of something big, and a lot of them are loosely based on the NLP box.

Worst case scenario: you've got ten minutes of your session left when your client remembers something which to them is truly awful. They are visibly distressed and tapping away, and you are bringing the SUDs down as fast as they will go, but your top priority is to get your client calm, grounded, focused, alert to their surroundings and fit to get up and leave and drive home safely, preferably without bursting into uncontrollable sobs later in the evening and deciding that all you did was take their money and make them feel worse than before.

So you've established that there is a thing or person in this scene they are recalling which they view as an absolute threat.

This is the one little skill that successfully uses breaking rapport to your client's personal advantage. If, after an hour of 'holding the space', being supportive and professional, you then, right when they feel upset, go and ask a quirky little question that seems to come out of nowhere, what this will achieve is startlingly effective.

There is no script. Here is the gist:

You to client: "Okay, so imagine a box."
Client: "D'wah?"
You (slowly!):

- Imagine a box.
- Can you see it?
- What colour is it?
- What is it made of?
- How strong is it?
- Make it stronger - how shall we do that?
- And stronger - what does that look like?
- And what is the lid like?
- Okay, so now I want you to put (the whole scene/event X./person Y/object Z) into the box.

- And shut the lid.
- And what shall we tie it up with?
- Anything stronger?
- What does it look, smell, feel like now?
- And how about a big chain and a big padlock?
- What does the key look like?
- Would you like to give the key to someone or put it somewhere safe?
- And where shall we put the box?
- And are you safe now?
- And is it safe to come back to the room?

Wait for an answer after each question. Make it a proper interaction and that's all there is. Just look at how many layers of safety you and your client have built between them and their issue. Obviously it remains unresolved, obviously it still needs work. This is an exercise in packing it back down, as near to airtight as you can get it for the time being, until there's a chance to continue the session.

The deal is: Box, stronger, lid, stronger, key, store key, store box, come back.

You need to take note of the whole description, but at very least the look and feel of the key and where the key and the box were stored, as these will be reminders and rapport builders also, when you return to retrieve the issue in your next session.

The box is a genius little creation. It starts by breaking a tiny little bit of rapport and in doing so helps the client to break state. They are forced to pay close attention to what you say next as you are no longer predictable. Then, whilst adding layers of safety between the client and the issue, the questions deliberately recruit all the senses so that they are focused on the box and not upon the upsetting situation.

You end up with the stressor safe inside an impermeable box, the box locked tight shut and stored somewhere really safe, the key somewhere else, just as safe, and the client feeling safe.

I love it. It is only one of many tools, but I hope it helps. You may find that when a memory is not so traumatic, any hesitation to leave the event or the younger self can be soothed by much smaller 'temporary fixes' which are limited only by the imagination. I find pink bubble wrap a very useful imaginary tool for holding or protecting any person in a scene so that the client feels they are safe to be left. The operative word is 'feel'. How your client feels about things, is after all the whole crux of the matter.

5.5

Recursion

This small section has been added to this book so that you can see how very easy it is to set up recursion in your own behaviours, instantly, or more deeply and longer term. I was tempted to rename this 'How to get hooked'.

The word recursive means repetitive, looping, recurring.

Recursion in Hypnotherapy:

In hypnotherapy, recursion is generally a 'good thing', being something that is deliberately encouraged by the practitioner to the benefit of the client. This is done by introducing a reward system so that behaviour A gets payoff B. More A = more B. One simple example, used earlier, is when the client is taken into a light trance only to be pulled sharply back out before being taken back in again, a system which is sometimes applied in order to get the client to a deeper state much more rapidly. This has the potential to be misused if not handled by a professional in the proper setting, as it relies on what NLP calls breaking rapport to set up a strong point of attraction, the little sister of a guiding star.

There is another way of achieving hypnotic recursion which is of great use when the client intends to return for further sessions. If a deeper trance results in a greater feeling of wellbeing when the client resurfaces, they will be more willing to go into a deep trance state the next time, and will find it easier to achieve.

The way that a hypnotherapist encourages this is quite crafty (meaning creative!). Yes, the sessions will achieve more in the given time if deep trance is achieved faster, as the induction and deepening protocols don't have to take so long. However, how relaxed and revitalised a client feels after a session has nothing to do with their actual presenting issue, such as weight loss, or smoking. In this instance it is all to do with the manner in which they are brought out of trance.

Inductions and deepeners can take more than half the session if a client is not used to the procedure but later on a simple suggestion is enough. Every time the client goes in they will naturally go in deeper and faster so more time is available for the session. A hypnotherapist can choose how much of that time they spend on the hypnotherapy itself (on the presenting issue) and how much on increasing feelings of wellbeing through the post hypnotic suggestion.

Perhaps because there is so much reliance on the process and on the skills of the therapist to induce a recursive state, in hypnotherapy 'Recursion' (almost a proper noun?) has come to simply mean 'repeated trance induction'.

Recursion in Psychology and Cognitive Behavioural Therapy:

In psychology and CBT, recursive is a word generally only used to describe pre-existing repetitive behaviours and repetitive thinking, i.e. NATs, negative automatic thoughts, also sometimes known as rumination or vicious circles. In other words, these are all 'not a good thing'. Formalised as a TLA, these behaviours are referred to as Recursive Cognitive Structures, basically 'things in your mind that keep looping'.

In this format, it can mean a self-fulfilling prophecy such as a fear that you will mess up, causing you to actually mess up, causing you to have even more fear next time etc.

In the same way that Maslow was modelling the behaviours of high achievers long before Grinder and Bandler did exactly the same to create NLP, so Henry Ford beat modern psychology to observing this condition when he rather neatly said, "Whether you think you can or think you can't, you're right."

Compulsion to Repeat and Guiding Stars:

Psychotherapy (or if you like long words, psychodynamic psychotherapy theory) uses the term 'compulsion to repeat' when referring to recursion built around deeply seated, long term unmet needs arising from early life.

When these become stronger over time the person eventually, compulsively, seeks out similar circumstances over and over again, still looking to have that original need met and healed. Dating someone like their mother or father is a commonly used example. Usually the need goes unmet again, and the belief becomes reinforced again.

Obviously this describes a foundational principle of EFT and Matrix Reimprinting, that all our current woes stem from beliefs and vows set up in early childhood. Using the same example, it means you could benefit someone's current relationships by bypassing them and working directly with their early events, but also you could niche 'boyfriend issues' (or any other issues) and know that, even if the work doesn't go back as far as childhood, you've still taken a big branch off that tree.

What if the compulsion to repeat was not simply due to a totally unmet need, but to one which was very nearly met? What if, just sometimes, this particular recursive loop or structure was established through a huge cosmic version of breaking rapport? Through having something that was longed for, snatched away at the last minute?

That's when we go running headlong back into limiting situations. These can be ones that feel very good to us and yet have a high price attached, or they can be more blatantly destructive. If your need was almost met in 'situation x'; if you had one brief, heady moment of feeling on top of the world, crucially of almost chucking away a truckload of judgments you'd made about your limitations or value, that can be enough to see you addicted to finishing the job.

If 'compulsion to repeat' is the drive to seek out certain situations, 'guiding stars' is a name that energists sometimes use for these sorts of initial events.

5.6

Rapport and Active Listening

Rapport is a state. It is the condition you arrive at when two people are in concordance with each other, safe and comfortable with each other and understood by each other. It is an indefinable sense of tribe.

Rapport cannot be faked, at least not often and not for long, although to hear some NLP trainers go on about it, you might think otherwise. All you can do is develop a set of manners and mannerisms which allow the other person to register that you appear to be on their level. These are all surface indicators; in my opinion they merely give people maximum opportunity to notice that you may be someone who truly understands them. That is the point where their sincerity radar fine tunes and does another sweep. When someone is enlivened and enthused by a potential connection between you, they naturally and easily pay you more attention. Fakery will show through.

Catching their attention in that way is the trick. When someone is feeling stressed, as you know, certain areas of their brain do not function to full capacity. The good news is that the part or parts which are charged with locating an exit route and establishing the nearest oasis of safety are still on the lookout. If you consistently mirror one or more of their behaviours such as stance, movement, breathing rate or opinion (by nodding or grunting to show agreement) in a way that is neither combative (don't shout at the shouter!) or mocking (do not exactly mimic or caricature) you will flag up as potentially representing all the safety and comfort of home.

Breaking rapport can be accidental, deliberate or reactive. It is usually uncomfortably confusing for the other person. Not only is the situation suddenly changed and strange and different; if rapport is a state in which we feel truly understood and safe enough to relax and drop any defensive behaviours, then breaking rapport is a cold, sharp shock to the system.

Making the client feel unsafe (failing to hold 'safe space' for them) is one way this can happen, as, obviously, is 'going where you don't belong'. Other ways rapport may be broken in a detrimental way during a session are listed in chapter 4 under 4.6 Swap Rules - How to play nicely with other people's children, and there are some more at the end of this current chapter.

Another mannerism that you will hear counsellors refer to as a listening skill is what they call reflecting, which means repeating back to someone the crucial elements of what they themselves have just said. This is done on the understanding that stressed people don't always register what just came out of their own mouths. Although we don't share the same terminology, you have already been trained to do the same through careful use of the client's own words when setting up a round of tapping and when clarifying and reframing.

Active listening is crucial.

Active listening has five key elements and again I think you'll soon realise that you have already covered this in your practice training, just in a different layout.

To be an active listener you need to:

1. Pay attention
2. Show that you are listening

3. Provide feedback
4. Defer judgment
5. Respond appropriately

In other words:
1. Look, listen, hear verbal and body language. Don't get distracted and don't start formulating a reply!
2. Nod, smile, encourage. If appropriate, mirror body language
3. Reflect back what they said, ask if you understood
4. Let them finish, don't interrupt, don't be focussed on making a counter argument
5. Be kind, polite, genuine, honest.

Obviously with the work that we do, there can be quite rapid progress with an issue, and we are constantly tapping, and would want to stop someone talking their way into overwhelm by getting them to tap and focus on one sensation or event as soon as possible!

Things that might break rapport and show bad listening skills in an energy therapy session could include:
1. An unsecured environment
2. Ill health, feeling out of your depth, feeling judgmental or any other situation which would stop a practitioner from being relaxed and fully attentive.
3. Making lots of notes, or fidgeting, or anything which concerns the client over whether they actually have your attention.
4. Becoming excited for the client, as this can make them feel 'on stage' as if there is potential for them to go wrong.

5. Making it obvious you think you can see where this is going. However positive this feels to you, it's another form of making a judgment and jumping to a conclusion. Perhaps you're right - accept that it's only a strong possibility, query whether you understand correctly and don't insult your client.

I'm sure you can add to that list!

6.

Postscript

Journal! Taking a snapshot

I admit it, my long term journal doesn't look like a book at all. It looks like a small, battered cardboard suitcase wedged at the back of a wardrobe.

In it are 'last' Christmas cards from people who have left this life, birthday cards to and from my children particularly from the first five years of their lives (the oldest two are now in their thirties) and secret letters, never sent, that describe all my early romances and the death of my first marriage, and a number of other, similar moments of extreme opinion. Beer stained or tear stained, it's somewhere in the case.

Unless it's in the shoebox. But that's another story.

Perhaps now if I suggest journaling or keeping some sort of diary, you will appreciate how loosely I use those terms.

I personally tried and failed to run a 'proper' journal several times during my early journey with energy therapy, returning to the idea every time something caused me to realise how much I'd grown and changed. The beauty of this lifestyle, this way of being, is that growth and realisation of potential are so rapid and yet so gentle. We sometimes have to 'see' the change on paper because we are unable to 'feel' it. The original state, the baseline from which we could measure a difference, has ceased to exist in our normal consciousness. We have to be consciously reminded.

What my efforts lacked was a template. I was going to say a plan, but that implies exertion and discipline. A template lets you off from most of the thinking and does away with the hesitation caused by a blank page. It removes any doubt, and speaking as someone who never knew whether to wax lyrical, engage in flights of fancy or purge the angsty depths of my newest project-for-change, I used to spend far too much time wondering what to write.

Here's the deal - there is no need to be all spiritual and open minded. Once every so often simply sit down and describe reality as you happen to find it. Better yet, make yourself a list of questions and answer the same ones, every single time. The only thing that needs to change is the date. Do not forget the date. I suggest these, although the right ones for you will be the right ones, for you. Go with your own flow!

- Who am I?
- Who am I really, underneath?
- What is my potential?
- What is my biggest regret?
- What is my biggest hope?
- If I were an angel or a perfect light being, what would be different about me?

What would be different about what I do next?

What then, when you've completed this exercise? Again that's up to you but I vote that you take the sheet you've worked on and tuck it away somewhere safe, somewhere you'll know to look for it next time the fancy takes you to repeat the process.

Enjoy! xx